Where Does Electricity Come From?

by C. Vance Cast
Illustrated by Sue Wilkinson

BARRON'S

Hi. I'm Clever Calvin.... We all use electricity every day, but we hardly ever stop to think about what it is or where it comes from.

Many things that are fun or useful in our lives need electricity in order to work—like computers, light bulbs, toasters, telephones, and refrigerators.

Even the machines that were used to make this book had to have electricity in order to work. But what is electricity? We can't see, feel, or hear it.

But we can see the light, feel the heat, and hear the sounds it makes. The word *electricity* is related to the word *electron*. Electrons are tiny particles found in everything—air, water, even rocks.

So electricity is all around us, but it does not usually
show itself. The tiny, crackling sparks you get when
you pet a cat on a cool, dry day tells you that electricity
is there.

Did you know that lightning is electricity too? It is!
In nature, there are many examples of electricity, and
lightning is probably one of the first that people
noticed.

Another example is the electric eel. The eel makes electricity in its muscles and uses it to shock other fish so they can't move. The eel can then escape from danger or easily catch its food.

All of these natural forms of electricity are very interesting, but none of them are useful. To turn a fan or run a computer, electricity must flow through a wire in a continuous stream called a *current.*

When you walk into a dark room and flip on a light switch, you put an electrical current to work. It makes the light glow for you. We know that electricity comes from sockets and outlets, but how does it get there in the first place? Where does it come from?

Plastic

Metal

Electrons

Electrical current is made in a power plant by machines called *generators*. Like this little hand-cranked model, generators have coils of wire that spin inside of magnets. When the coils spin, the magnets force the electrons in the wire to move, producing a current.

Something must make the coils in the generator turn. This is done with a *turbine* that is connected to the generator. Turbines are large wheels that have fins or blades. Some look like giant fans or pinwheels.

When something moves through the turbine, it pushes the blades, making the turbine turn. There are many things that can be used to do this—water, steam, and wind are just a few of them.

First, let's see how water is used to do this. Many electric power plants are built near waterfalls, fast-moving rivers, or dams. These are called *hydroelectric* plants. Hydro is from an ancient Greek word that means water.

Generator

Turbine

When water is released through a pipe in the dam, the blades of the turbine catch the water, and the turbine goes round and round. It works exactly the same way with a waterfall or even a swiftly flowing river.

Some power plants use steam to turn the turbines. This kind of plant is called a *thermal* power plant. Coal, oil, or gas is burned in a large furnace to make the steam.

The large furnace heats giant boilers filled with water.
As the water boils, it makes the steam, which is
released to turn the turbine.

Another way to make steam is with nuclear energy. In a *nuclear* power plant, a nuclear reactor is used to split the atoms of a mineral called *uranium*. This produces the heat needed to boil the water.

A piece of uranium about the size of the bell on my bicycle can give as much heat as a pile of coal bigger than a house. Unfortunately, the uranium gives off dangerous particles. This is called *radioactivity*. Disposing of radioactive wastes safely is a major problem.

The sun also is used to heat water into steam. This is called *solar* power—from *sol*, the Latin word for sun. The sun's light is collected by *solar cells*, but because most solar cells can only collect small amounts of energy, they are not used very widely.

Now, once it's generated, how does all this electricity get to your house and mine? Sometimes the electricity is made in a power plant near your town, but sometimes it is made hundreds of miles away.

But no matter where it is made, the power plant sends very high powered electricity through thick wires called *transmission lines*. These wires are strung on tall, metal towers called *pylons*.

The pylons lead to huge *transformers* that change the electricity into a form that is the right power for our homes. When the electricity leaves the transformers, it is carried by smaller wires.

These wires are strung on wooden poles. You see these
poles in your neighborhood by the side of the road.
You may even like to count them during long trips.

It is usually these poles that bring the electricity to your house. Then you can use it for whatever you need—light, heat, motion, or sound.

In many big cities some of the wires are underground. They are wrapped together in special covering to protect them and then buried under the streets in concrete pipes. These are underground cables.

Whether the electricity comes to your house by poles or underground cable, it goes to a little box that has dials behind a glass window. This box is the electric *meter* and it measures how much electricity you use. A meter reader checks it about once a month; then the electric company sends you a bill.

Did you know that electricity helps make our cars move? It also is used to make the horn blow, the radio play, and the headlights light up.

No, we don't have to plug the car into an electrical outlet. It runs with the help of a *battery*, where the electricity is stored. The car's engine runs on gasoline, but the electricity from the battery is what starts the engine and keeps the gasoline burning.

Unlike the batteries in a toy or a flashlight, this battery takes a long time to run out of electricity. This is because there is also a generator in the car. When the car engine is running, it turns the generator—making more electricity to store in the battery.

People have been interested in electricity for thousands of years. Long ago, they found shiny, yellow rocks that looked like glass. These rocks really were hardened tree sap called *amber*.

The people thought there was magic in these rocks because when the amber was rubbed on fur, something very strange happened. The rock would pick up feathers and bits of grass.

Of course today, we know that wasn't magic. It was the static electricity. You can do the same thing they did. Here is an experiment you can do to make your own static electricity.

First you will need a balloon. Blow up the balloon and tie a knot in the neck.

Rub the balloon on a dry towel
or on your clothes. Now
the balloon has static
electricity. Let's see
what we can do
with it.

Put the balloon against the wall. It should stay
there all by itself for a little while.

Now cut some small pieces of paper and put them on a table. Rub the balloon just as you did before.

This time hold the balloon over the paper.
Watch the pieces jump
up and fall down
from the balloon.

Now rub the balloon on your hair, then hold the balloon a few inches from your head. Does your hair rise up and go toward the balloon the way mine does?

That was fun. I hope you learned a little about electricity and where it comes from. Bye for now.

Electricity is useful and good—but only if it is used carefully. Here are a few safety tips from Clever Calvin. You can ask your parents to talk about them with you.

Don't spill water on anything electrical—even if it is on fire.

Don't touch anything electrical with wet hands, when in the bathtub, or when standing on a wet floor.

Don't poke anything (except electrical plugs) into electrical wall outlets.

Don't cut or break or play with electrical wires.

Don't use anything electrical if the wires are torn or broken.

Don't touch the insides of a television, toaster, or anything electrical.

Don't go near outdoor electric wires that are lying on the ground.

Don't go near water or stand under a tree when there is a lightning storm. Go inside.

Glossary

amber A hard, pale yellow, reddish, or brownish stone formed from the sap of prehistoric pine trees.

battery A unit that produces an electric current by a chemical process.

current The flow or movement of electricity in a certain direction.

electron A tiny particle that carries a charge of electricity.

generator A machine that converts mechanical energy into electrical energy. A dynamo.

hydroelectricity Electric current produced by the energy of moving water.

meter (electric) An instrument that measures and records the amount of electricity passing through it.

nuclear Having to do with the center or *nucleus* of an atom.

pylon A metal tower supporting electric power lines.

radioactivity The throwing off of high-energy units by elements such as uranium.

solar Having to do with the sun, such as the production of electric current by the sun's energy.

solar cell A unit that collects and converts sunlight into electricity.

thermal Having to do with heat, such as in the production of electric current by heating water to make steam.

transformer A unit that changes an electrical current from high to low voltage or vice versa.

transmission line Thick wire that carries high-powered electricity from one point to another.

turbine A kind of engine that delivers power produced by the flow of steam, air, or water against curved blades attached to a central rod (or rotor).

uranium A radioactive metallic element.

© Copyright 1992 by Barron's Educational Series, Inc.
250 Wireless Boulevard
Hauppauge, NY 11788

International Standard Book No. 0-8120-4835-0

Library of Congress Catalog Card No. 91-46472

PRINTED IN HONG KONG

2345   4900   987654321

Library of Congress Cataloging-in-Publication Data
Cast, C. Vance.
  Where does electricity come from? / by C. Vance Cast ; illustrated by Sue Wilkinson.
  Summary: Explains, in simple terms, what electricity is and how it is generated.
  ISBN 0-8120-4835-0
  1. Electricity—Juvenile literature.
[1. Electricity.] I. Wilkinson, Sue (Susan), ill. II. Title.
QC527.2.C3755   1992
537—dc20   91-46472